THE GULF OF MEXICO
OIL SPILL

Essential Events

THE GULF OF MEXICO
OIL SPILL

BY COURTNEY FARRELL

Content Consultant
Ian MacDonald
Department of Oceanography
Florida State University

ABDO
Publishing Company

CREDITS

Published by ABDO Publishing Company, 8000 West 78th Street, Edina, Minnesota 55439. Copyright © 2011 by Abdo Consulting Group, Inc. International copyrights reserved in all countries. No part of this book may be reproduced in any form without written permission from the publisher. The Essential Library™ is a trademark and logo of ABDO Publishing Company.

Printed in the United States of America,
North Mankato, Minnesota
112010
012011

 THIS BOOK CONTAINS AT LEAST 10% RECYCLED MATERIALS.

Editor: Jill Sherman
Interior Design and Production: Kazuko Collins
Cover Design: Marie Tupy

Library of Congress Cataloging-in-Publication Data
Farrell, Courtney.
  The Gulf of Mexico oil spill / by Courtney Farrell.
    p. cm. -- (Essential events)
  Includes bibliographical references and index.
  ISBN 978-1-61714-765-4
  1. BP Deepwater Horizon Explosion and Oil Spill, 2010. 2. Oil spills--Mexico, Gulf of--Psychological aspects. 3. Underwater explosions--Mexico, Gulf of. 4. Oil spills--Environmental aspects--Mexico, Gulf of. I. Title.
  TD427.P4F365 2011
  363.738'20916364--dc22
                                        2010044976

TABLE OF CONTENTS

The US Coast Guard attempts to burn off oil leaking from the sunken oil rig Deepwater Horizon.

CATASTROPHE ON THE DEEPWATER HORIZON

ike Williams, a big redheaded man, was the chief electronics technician on the oil rig Deepwater Horizon. The oil rig was a state-of-the-art wonder, a $350 million city on the sea. It was as big as two football fields put together, and its structure soared 378 feet (115 m) above the waves. The 126 crew members even had their own movie theater and bowling alley on board. At night, the rig was a thing of beauty, its golden lights shining like jewels on the dark water. But on April 20, 2010, those lights would be extinguished.

Williams first knew something was wrong when he noticed the engine noises. Williams recalled that night saying, "I'm hearing hissing. Engines are over-revving. And then all of a sudden, all the lights in my shop just started getting brighter and brighter and brighter. And I knew then something bad was getting ready to happen."[1]

The Deepwater Horizon was operating in the Gulf of Mexico, about 40 miles (64 km) southeast of the Louisiana coastline. About 10:00 p.m. on April 20, explosive methane gas began to escape from the well. As safety measures called for, a warning system was in place to alert the crew of an emergency. But no warning bell rang. The system had been disabled because false alarms

The Companies Involved

The Deepwater Horizon was owned by a company called Transocean Ltd., but it was leased to BP. (BP once stood for British Petroleum, but the company now uses just its initials.) Other companies were involved as well. Halliburton Energy Services had the contract for cementing the well, and Cameron International Corporation had manufactured the wellhead safety equipment.

sometimes disturbed the crew, who spent their days and nights on the rig. No one knew there was a problem until it was too late.

Offshore Drilling Rigs

Many of the world's richest remaining oil deposits are under the seafloor, making them difficult and dangerous to reach. A variety of mobile drilling platforms have been invented to access subsea reserves. Among them are drilling barges—floating platforms made to collect oil from deposits under calm, shallow waters. Another design is the jack-up rig, which comes equipped with long legs that drop to reach the seafloor. A submersible rig rests on barges that float to the site. The barges then are filled with water so they sink, forming a stable surface for the stilts that hold a platform above the surface.

None of these rigs are made for use in extremely deep water. Deepwater petroleum deposits must be reached via semisubmersible rigs, such as the Deepwater Horizon. Semisubmersible rigs can be used in water up to 10,000 feet (3,000 m) deep. Once the rig is towed into position, water is let in to partially fill the lower hull. This stabilizes the rig, letting it float low in the water.

The Deepwater Horizon used a satellite positioning system and thrusters to maintain its position over the well. The deposit this rig was trying to tap at the time of the accident was 13,000 feet (4,000 m) below the seabed of the Gulf of Mexico, in 5,000 feet (1,500 m) of water.

Undersea oil deposits are under immense pressure. So when the well blew, the methane did not bubble up gently. Instead, it rocketed toward the surface in a giant expanding bubble. When it reached the rig, fumes shot out and jetted violently across the decks. It took only the slightest spark to ignite them. Fires broke out. The fire was fueled by an endless supply of oil and gas streaming from the undersea well. Finally, alarm sirens began to scream.

The engines that ran the rig's generator began to race as gas fumes surrounded them. The engines picked up speed. They became so loud that they almost drowned out the siren. The rig's electric system could not take the load. The electricity surged, and lightbulbs started popping all around the room. Williams was just getting up from his desk to investigate when his computer monitor exploded. He ran for the engine room, which was enclosed behind three-inch- (8-cm-) thick steel fire doors.

Williams recalled:

> As I reach for the handle, I heard this awful hissing noise, this whoosh. . . . And, at the height of the hiss, a huge explosion. The explosion literally rips the door from the hinges, hits, impacts me and takes me to the other side of the shop. And I'm up against a wall, when I finally come around, with a door on top of me. And I remember thinking to myself, "You know, this, this is it. I'm gonna die right here."[2]

Mike Williams is a powerful man, and he needed every ounce of his strength to free himself from beneath the heavy blast door. It was all the injured man could do just to crawl across the floor. But just as he reached the next steel door, an explosion blew it off as well. As Williams recounted, the force of the blast "took me, the door, and slid me about 35 feet [10 m] backwards again. And planted me up against another wall."[3]

At that point, Williams knew there was nothing he could do for the engines; they were destroyed. The air in his workshop was choked with smoke and carbon dioxide from the fire suppressor. He could not breathe. His forehead had been slashed, and blood was running into his eyes. That was when Williams decided, "I'm going to get outside. I may die out there, but I'm gonna get outside."[4]

Into the Fire

Out on deck, Williams grabbed a life jacket and looked around. Through the smoke, he saw destruction all around. Fires burned and a couple of lifeboats were already leaving. Two more lifeboats were available, but Williams remembered his training and turned away. He was supposed to report to the bridge in an emergency.

Visiting Executives Are Injured in the Accident

At the time of the accident, BP executives were visiting the Deepwater Horizon to hold an award ceremony honoring the crew for its outstanding safety record. The executives were injured during the disaster, but they all survived. Eleven crew members died.

On the bridge, Captain Curt Kuchta confirmed that he had given the order to abandon ship. Approximately ten members of the bridge crew were left. They were trying to activate emergency systems designed to stopper the well and choke off the flow of fuel to the fire. The emergency systems failed. They had lost propulsion. There was no way to get the burning rig away from the fuel that continued to gush out of the well. The Deepwater Horizon was doomed.

Andrea Fleytas, a 23-year-old navigation worker, was one of only three women on the rig. She realized suddenly that no call for help had been sent. Fleytas grabbed the radio.

"Mayday, Mayday. This is Deepwater Horizon. We have an uncontrollable fire."[5]

"I didn't give you authority to do that," Captain Kuchta snapped.[6]

"I'm sorry," Andrea responded.[7]

But Andrea should not have been sorry; that distress call probably saved more than 100 lives.

Williams left the bridge and made his way toward the lifeboats. Around him, fires raged and occasional explosions rocked the dying rig.

"It's just take-your-breath-away type explosions, shake your body to the core explosions. Take your vision away from the percussion of the explosions," Williams recalled.[8]

WILLIAMS MAKES HIS ESCAPE

In the few minutes it had taken Williams to cross the bridge, the last lifeboats departed. But Williams, the captain, and the bridge crew were still on board. They had been abandoned by frightened crew members rushing to escape. At that point, approximately eight people were left on the rig. There was one boat left—a small inflatable one. The group rushed to inflate it and load a wounded man on board. The heat from the fire was intense, and Williams feared the rubber boat would melt or pop.

They were having trouble launching the boat, which was being lowered toward the water on ropes.

The Truth about BP's Safety Record

Despite its cheery yellow and green flower logo, international oil giant BP is far from green. OSHA (Occupational Safety and Health Administration) has fined the British-based corporation 760 times for violations that resulted in injuries, deaths, and damage to the environment in the company's refinery operations. In October 2009, BP was fined a record $50 million in criminal fines connected to the accident at its Texas refinery, where an explosion killed 15 people and injured another 180.

In 2006, one of BP's pipelines in Alaska ruptured due to poor maintenance. It spilled thousands of gallons of oil onto the tundra. No one was injured, but the cleanup took months. BP had earlier paid fines for dumping harmful chemicals on Alaska's North Slope.

Mike Williams recounts events that took place on the day of the explosion.

While they waited for their turns to board, Williams, Fleytas, and another crewman took shelter from the heat behind a wall. Suddenly, the ropes loosened and the rubber boat lurched toward the water. Without power to the rig, there was no way to winch it up again. They were left behind.

**What Happened
to the Captain?**

Captain Kuchta was not on board the rubber raft when it was launched. After the raft launched, he leaped off the rig into the water. He then swam to the boat, only to find it still attached to the burning rig by a rope. Captain Kuchta swam to another craft for a knife, swam back, and freed the raft, saving the men on board.

It was a ten-story drop to the sea. From that height, the density of the water makes it hard enough to snap an arm or a leg on impact. As the fire burned out of control behind him, Williams knew that if he did not jump, he would die.

"We're gonna burn up. Or we're gonna jump," he told Fleytas.[9]

What Williams did not know was that an oil slick floated on the water below, and it was burning.

Deepwater Horizon burns into the night.

Survivors of the explosion were evacuated to hospitals.

A Long, Slow Rescue

*A*s Deepwater Horizon burned behind him, Chief Electronics Technician Mike Williams took a desperate leap into the waters of the Gulf of Mexico. As Williams recalled, "I made those three steps, and I pushed off the end of the rig. And I fell for what seemed like forever."[1]

When Williams surfaced, he became coated in oil. He began to swim frantically away from the rig, trying to escape the pain. He kept swimming until he lost all sensation and floated in the dark ocean. The silence was so complete that Williams wondered if he was dead. That was when he heard the voice of his rescuer, who pulled him into the safety of a small boat. The boat turned out to be from a supply vessel, the *Damon B. Bankston*, which was tethered to the rig at the time of the blast.

Williams was frightened, exhausted, and covered in oil, but he was safe. As it turned out, Williams's survival would prove crucial to the investigation of the accident. Williams's testimony would later clarify exactly what went wrong—and who was responsible.

How Andrea Fleytas Survived

Williams figured Fleytas must have jumped from the rig, because the boat that rescued him pulled her from the water next. Actually, she never had to take that leap. The quick-thinking Fleytas jumped into the rubber life raft as it was descending.

The raft was tangled in ropes. When it drifted under the burning rig, Andrea bailed out. "All I saw was smoke and fire," she recalled. "I swam away from the rig for my life."[2] The boat that rescued her and Williams also rescued the trapped raft, saving the passengers.

DELAYED RESCUE

On the night of the accident, helicopters evacuated the most seriously wounded men to nearby hospitals. But the helicopters did not return immediately for the other stranded crew members. Survivors said they were kept on the water for 15 hours after the 10:00 p.m. evacuation. Lifeboats were ordered to remain nearby the Deepwater Horizon. The men and women in them had to sit for hours watching their burning rig. This was no ordinary fire. The

Post-Traumatic Stress Disorder (PTSD)

Post-traumatic stress disorder, or PTSD, is an anxiety disorder that may occur as a result of a traumatic experience. Symptoms include flashbacks, or vivid, spontaneous recollections of the stressful event. Sufferers may also have some or all of the following symptoms: heart palpitations, avoidance of things that remind them of the traumatic event, emotional numbness, difficulty concentrating, difficulty sleeping, and anxiety or agitation.

PTSD varies in the intensity of its symptoms. For example, a soldier with extreme PTSD may hear a popping balloon and dive for cover, momentarily reliving the memory of a battle. When the flashback is over, he realizes where he is and that his reaction was unnecessary.

A survivor of a dangerous accident may have a more mild form of PTSD. For instance, people who have been in car accidents often report feeling nervous during subsequent car trips.

People who all survive the same disaster do not all develop PTSD. Some people are more resilient—are able to resist the effects of stress. Experts think that loving relationships increase resilience. A history of trauma does the opposite, as survivors of multiple disasters are more likely to develop PTSD. The disorder can be treated with therapy, antidepressants, and sedatives.

flames were 200 to 300 feet (60 to 90 m) high, and they could be seen for 35 miles (56 km).

"Talking about adding to post-traumatic stress. Don't take them in once you get 'em off the rig. Just keep 'em there for 15 hours so that they can watch, watch their rig burning up, knowing they had to leave some of those guys behind," pointed out Kurt Arnold, attorney for one of the survivors.[3]

When the survivors were finally rescued, they had been awake now for more than 40 hours. It had been 29 hours since the fire. They were then transported by bus to a nearby hotel. They were not allowed to see or speak to their families, their lawyers, or the press. Instead, Transocean investigators and consultants presented crew members with forms to sign before they were allowed to sleep or speak to waiting family members. Many of the stressed workers initialed the forms, which stated that they were not witnesses to the accident, had no personal knowledge about the incident, and were not injured. In many cases this was not true.

COAST GUARD LAUNCHES RESCUE

There was no delay from the US Coast Guard, which responded immediately to the disaster. The

The Victims of Deepwater Horizon

The names of the victims of the Deepwater Horizon accident are listed below.
- Jason Anderson, 35, of Midfield, Texas.
- Aaron Dale Burkeen, 37, of Philadelphia, Mississippi.
- Donald Clark, 49, of Newellton, Louisiana.
- Stephen Ray Curtis, 39, of Georgetown, Louisiana.
- Roy Wyatt Kemp, 27, of Jonesville, Louisiana.
- Karl Kleppinger Jr., 38, of Natchez, Mississippi.
- Gordon Jones, 28, of Baton Rouge, Louisiana.
- Keith Blair Manuel, 56, of Gonzales, Louisiana.
- Dewey Revette, 48, of State Line, Mississippi.
- Shane Roshto, 22, of Liberty, Mississippi.
- Adam Weise, 24, of Yorktown, Texas.

Coast Guard is a branch of the US military. It is perhaps best known for its search-and-rescue missions.

While the survivors waited on lifeboats, Coast Guard vessels were out searching for anyone who might have been lost in the water. In total, there were 11 missing men. The Coast Guard ran 17 search-and-rescue missions after the accident: 12 using planes and helicopters and five using boats. The Coast Guard did not abandon the rescue effort until April 23, when there was virtually no chance of finding a survivor. No bodies were ever recovered.

In June, two months after the accident, US President Barack Obama invited the victims' families to meet with him privately at the White House. He expressed his condolences and asked for their input on preventing future oil rig disasters.

The US Coast Guard searched for the 11 missing workers for three days.

*Interior Secretary Ken Salazar asks safety questions
on the drilling floor of an oil rig in the Gulf of Mexico.*

DEEPWATER DRILLING

*D*rilling for oil is dangerous work. It
requires specialized equipment and
careful monitoring. Deepwater drilling can be
especially difficult because of the challenges of
drilling 10,000 feet (3,000 m) beneath the ocean.

Deepwater drill rigs use 30-foot (9-m) sections of pipe, which are threaded to screw together to form one immensely long pipe called the drill string. The drill string drops to the ocean floor through a flexible tube called a marine riser. At the bottom of the drill string is a rotating drill bit. As the drill bit digs deeper, new sections of pipe are added to the top. The subsea well is lined with sections of metal pipe called casing that are cemented into place.

Mud is pumped down through a hollow pipe to lubricate the rotating drill and remove debris from the bottom of the well. Mud is important in sealing the well and preventing methane gas from rising out of it.

Oil wells contain a mixture of oil, water, and various flammable gases. If not tapped properly, the contents would shoot out of the well with incredible force. Pressure must be applied to control the oil deposits below. To control the pressure, wells are capped with three concrete plugs. When it is time to pump out the oil,

Mud

Drilling mud is a viscous liquid. It is made from a mixture of clay, water, and other chemicals. Mud is pumped down through the drill pipe to pool around the drill bit. It comes back up through the space between the pipe and the wall of the borehole. It circulates constantly this way. Rock fragments sheared off by the drill often become suspended in the mud. They are filtered out at the surface. The heavy liquid is important in drilling safety. It helps keep flammable gas from rising out of the well. Instruments scan mud for the presence of gas, and alarms should warn workers if unsafe levels are detected.

explosives are sent down to fracture the concrete. This allows oil to rise up slowly through the cracks in the concrete, making the pressure easier to control.

THE BLOWOUT PREVENTER

A blowout occurs when gas pressure inside the well is not properly controlled. The pressure can force reservoir liquids (seawater, oil, or gas) up the well column. In the ground, gas is under pressure, so it is compressed. Gas expands as it rises toward the surface. It can accelerate to almost supersonic speeds. Devices called blowout preventers (BOPs) are intended to

Oil Field Gushers

The oil industry began in earnest in the late 1800s, before technology existed to control pressure from erupting oil wells. In those early years, striking oil might mean a gusher— a geyser of oil that shoots high into the air. Gushers could shoot 200 feet (61 m) or higher. Black-and-white photographs depict grimy men celebrating under black fountains of oil.

Gushers have come to represent the thrill of striking it rich. However, oil field gushers were quite dangerous and wasteful. The explosive force could kill workers who were near the well. And the thunderous sound of the eruption deafened some survivors. Gushers also frequently destroyed nearby equipment. Fire during a blowout was another serious risk. The oil that soaked the land could ignite, causing a fast-spreading fire.

Also, as the uncapped oil sprayed over the land, it became nearly impossible to retrieve those thousands of barrels worth of oil. The environmental impact of oil soaking the ground was not well understood in those days. Today, sites of old oil field gushers remain toxic.

stop this from happening. They help control the oil. BOPs are very important during emergencies when well pressure cannot be controlled. Companies do not want to lose any of the oil they are collecting. Lost oil means lost profits for companies. It is also bad news for the environment.

The BOP sits at the wellhead on the bottom of the ocean. It is a huge, 450-short ton (408-t) structure, as tall as a house, containing valves and hydraulic pistons. The BOP is used to test the pressure inside a well. In an emergency, it should also stop oil and methane gas from escaping. The drill passes through a tunnel in the BOP on its way to the well. Inside the tunnel, the space around the drill pipe can be sealed by a rubber gasket called an annular. When closed, the annular fits tightly around the drill pipe, holding oil and bubbles of methane safely inside the well.

An accident involving the BOP on Deepwater Horizon occurred on March 20, four weeks prior to the explosion. During a routine pressure

The Blowout Preventer

Operators on the rig control the blowout preventer with two pods that are connected to the surface by wires. In an emergency, hydraulic rams can slide in from each side, closing a rubber seal across the pipe. Oil should never be able to escape from the well, even during a catastrophe like the one on April 20, 2010. In a last-ditch effort to prevent oil from gushing into the ocean, a shearing ram should be triggered inside the BOP. This seals off the well, destroying and capping it at the same time.

A blowout preventer is used to control the pressure of oil while drilling.

test, the annular (the seal that keeps methane from erupting out of the well) was closed tightly around the drill pipe. But someone accidentally bumped a joystick. Fifteen feet (4.5 m) of pipe were dragged upward through the closed rubber seal. The force partially fragmented the seal. Later, chunks of rubber came up in the mud.

A concerned worker brought fistfuls of rubber to show to senior subsea supervisor Mark Hay. But, according to Williams, Hay said that the rubber was "no big deal."[1] This was a critical error. If the annular had been intact, it could have stopped gas from rising out of the well.

A Dangerous Formation

The well the Deepwater Horizon was drilling was in a particularly dangerous formation in the Gulf of Mexico. It is called the Macondo Prospect. Undersea oil deposits are normally under pressure due to the weight of the water and rock above them. Because of its great depth, the pressure on this well was even more extreme than typical underwater drilling sites. Large quantities of gas were also present.

BP and Transocean bosses knew that the Macondo Prospect formation was a tricky one. One attempt to drill into it had already failed. This failed attempt had cost BP $25 million. As Williams tells it, the problem with the first well began when it took longer than planned to reach the oil. The drilling had

"The Well from Hell"

The word *kick* is oil field jargon for a sudden increase in pressure when a gas bubble rises up out of the well. The Macondo well kicked so hard and so often that it worried the crew, who nicknamed it "the well from hell." The BOP and the mud inside the well are able to control most kicks. But if they are not controlled, a huge belch of methane could be released and ignited—exactly what happened on the Deepwater Horizon.

fallen three weeks behind schedule. It cost BP $1 million a day to operate the rig and its supply ships.

The drill crew was instructed to increase drilling speed. But increasing speed also increases the chance of other risks. BP's decision to increase drilling speed proved to be a mistake. The well could not take the added force. It shattered, and the drill bit became irretrievably stuck. The pipe had to be cut, and the crew had no choice but to leave the expensive drill bit behind. This path to the oil was now blocked. And a new well would have to be dug.

Restarting the drill also meant that workers would be under more pressure than ever to finish the job quickly. According to Williams, "There was gonna be a push coming; a push to pick up production and pick up the pace."[2]

BP and Transocean denied pushing workers to take risks. They say safety is a priority, and every worker has stop work authority.

The Deepwater Horizon blowout preventer is lifted onto the deck of the Helix Q4000 in the Gulf of Mexico near the coast of Louisiana.

US Coast Guard Captain Hung Nguyen questions BP officials during the investigation in August 2010 in Houston, Texas.

RISKING LIVES FOR PROFIT

*I*n the aftermath of the explosion, two issues took priority—capping the well that was allowing oil to gush into the Gulf of Mexico and investigating the cause of the explosion. Investigators needed to determine what went wrong in BP's operation. Could the explosion of Deepwater Horizon have been prevented? And, if so, who exactly was to blame?

It did not take long before BP's questionable cost-cutting methods came to light. Interviews with survivors helped piece together the story of what went wrong on April 20. And further investigations into the company's practices would reveal that safety often took a backseat to speed when it came to drilling.

An official investigation into the accident began in May 2010. The US Coast Guard and the Bureau of Ocean Energy Management, Regulation and Enforcement held joint hearings to investigate the accident. Congress soon began its own investigation. Top executives from all the companies involved were questioned extensively. Throughout the testimony, one underlying theme became clear: a corporate culture that was willing to risk lives for profit.

Workers Feared Reprisals for Whistle-Blowing

Prior to the accident on Deepwater Horizon, Transocean circulated a safety survey among its employees. The results indicated that about half of their employees were concerned about safety practices on board the rig but were afraid of reprisals if they spoke up. They were also concerned about neglected equipment.

Officials with the Coast Guard and the Interior Department's
Minerals Management Service take an oath before
holding a joint hearing on May 11, 2010.

THE NEGATIVE PRESSURE TEST

The rig was nearing the end of the drilling
process when the accident occurred. Once drilling
reached the oil lying 13,000 feet (4,000 m) below
the seabed, the crew was supposed to cap the well.
Then they would be finished with the job. It was
during the capping process that the explosion
happened.

On April 17, drilling on the well was finished,
and it was then lined with steel and cement. By
April 20, two of the three giant 300-foot (91-km)
concrete plugs had already been installed. These plugs
are meant to hold down the pressurized contents of
the well. They would remain in place until BP could

return to begin oil production. The crew would never get the chance to install the third plug.

The final step before capping a well is to test the pressure inside it. This test is to make sure that no gas is leaking in from surrounding formations. During a negative pressure test, the fluid pressure in the well is reduced by removing some of the mud and replacing it with seawater. The pressure in the well is then monitored for half an hour. If the pressure rises, it means that the well did not seal properly. Gas could be entering the line from the surrounding formation.

Who Is in Charge Here?

During an 11:00 a.m. meeting on the day of the explosion, top officials from BP and Transocean argued about how best to do this negative pressure test. Normally, drilling crews take out only about 300 feet (91 m) worth of the mud in a well. This is because the lighter seawater cannot hold down gas as well as mud can. Until workers are sure the well is

The Death of a Peacemaker

After the argument between Transocean and BP officials, Dewey Revette tried to calm down the angry crew members. The crew was upset with BP's decision to remove extra mud for the pressure test. Revette told the other men, "We'll get it worked out. Let's get up there and go to work."[1] Revette was one of the 11 men who died in the accident.

sealed, they do not dare remove much more mud.
Transocean's chief mechanic Douglas H. Brown
attended the meeting on April 20. According to
Brown, the BP plan was to remove ten times more
drilling mud than usual from the well before doing
the test. This would speed up the process of finishing
the well. This way, BP could begin removing oil
and the Deepwater Horizon could get to its next
job faster. Though it was risky to remove so much
mud for the test, BP representative Donald Vidrine
insisted on it.

Harrell Saw It Coming

As the meeting about
the pressure test was
concluded, rig manager
Jimmy Wayne Harrell
was heard saying, "I guess
that's what we have those
pinchers for."[3]

Pinchers are fail-safe
devices on blowout pre-
venters. In an emergency,
giant hydraulic pinchers
should cut the pipe, stop-
ping the flow of oil and
gas to the surface. It seems
that Harrell believed BP's
plan was unsafe and
could result in a blowout.

"The company man was basically
saying, 'This is how it's gonna be,'"
Douglas Brown testified before the
joint panel.[2] According to Brown,
a number of Transocean employees
disagreed with BP's decision,
including rig manager Jimmy Wayne
Harrell, tool pusher Miles Randall
Ezell, and the rig's primary driller,
Dewey Revette. Donald Vidrine
was the "company man" on the rig,
responsible for conveying orders
from the BP office in Houston,
Texas. Despite the objections of the

Transocean men, BP had the lease on the rig, so Vidrine's orders prevailed.

When the pressure tests were run, the initial result showed that the well was not stable. The tests were rerun several times because the results were difficult to interpret. A number of tests were done, but they all showed unclear results. At about 8:00 p.m., another test was run. This time, the well was declared to pass, just two hours before the explosion.

Shifting the Blame

As the investigation continued, the companies and their lawyers maneuvered, trying to shift blame onto each other. BP blamed Transocean for defects in the blowout preventer. Transocean accused Halliburton of doing a shoddy job of cementing the well. BP claimed that the cement Halliburton used was unstable, allowing gas to enter the well.

Halliburton said that BP did not flush the well with drilling fluid before cementing, as recommended. Halliburton technical adviser Jesse Gagliano testified that he had warned BP officials that gas would enter the well unless BP used more centralizers. Centralizers are devices that keep the pipe centered in the hole. BP failed to follow instructions, using only six of the 21 recommended centralizers.

The media and the public were following the hearings closely. They were interested in finding out exactly what had gone wrong on Deepwater Horizon. But it seemed that everyone had an excuse for his or her failures and were blaming each other for poor construction. Even President Obama was fed up, stating, "I did not appreciate what I considered to be a ridiculous spectacle during the congressional hearings into this matter. You had executives of BP and Transocean and Halliburton falling over each other to point the finger of blame at somebody else."[4]

Nine Men Died Trying to Save the Rig

The trouble began at around 10:00 p.m. Jason Anderson, a 35-year-old father of two from Texas, was supervising an eight-man crew on the drilling floor. The drilling floor is up on the highest of the rig's three decks. Though there was a pressure surge from the well, no alarm warned the men about gas on the deck. The pressure meant that methane was rising out of the well column.

The men knew they were in danger. Company guidelines required them to consult two senior officials before making a decision about how to proceed. The men made four calls to senior officials, including Donald Vidrine and Transocean's installation manager Jimmy Harrell. In one of these calls, the drill crew reported that they were getting mud back.

Mud spurting from the well indicated that a lot of gas was rising fast. But without a gas alarm, most of the rig's crew did not know there was a problem.

Unclear Test Results

In one of the repeat tests, pressure was high in the main pipe. This could mean that gas had leaked into the well. However, there was no pressure in two other lines. Pressure should be the same in all three lines. Investigators later learned this was because of problems with the plumbing of the BOP. But at the time, it made the trouble in the well difficult to identify.

Such an alarm would have signaled everyone on board the rig about the gas. They could have then turned off pilot lights and doused any other flames that could ignite the gas.

Anderson and his men worked furiously, trying to control the surge by closing the bag—a seal meant to stop gas movement. But their equipment was faulty and the attempt to seal off the gas failed. That was when gas alarms finally began to sound on the deck. But it was too late. The men were working next to the pipe that connected the rig to the well. When a jet of burning gas shot out of the well, Anderson and eight other men were incinerated.

Managers were racing to the drilling floor when the fire broke out. They only survived because the fire erupted before they got there, driving them back with its intense heat. Harrell was in the shower at the time of the accident. Two explosions blew the walls and ceiling off his bathroom. He dressed in the rubble and ran for the bridge where he rapidly checked instrument panels. Indicators there showed that the BOP had failed. Under 5,000 feet (1,500 m) of water, oil was already escaping from beneath the seafloor.

Mike Williams testifies that the alarms were disabled on Deepwater Horizon.

During the last shore leave before his death, Jason Anderson visited his father, Billy Anderson. According to Billy Anderson, during that visit Jason told him that BP was pressuring workers to take risks in order to speed up drilling. Other employees have echoed this claim. But the company denies having pressured workers to neglect safety.

"My boy was cremated," said Billy Anderson. "But the actions he and those other 10 heroes took are what made it possible for more than 100 other people to escape with their lives."[5]

The Alarms Were Silenced

At the joint hearings, Williams testified along with other employees and company officials from Transocean and BP. Williams and his supervisor, chief engineer Stephen Bertone, explained that the alarm, which would have warned the crew of gas on the deck, was deliberately bypassed. The alarm systems were set to "inhibited," meaning they could continue to sense gas levels but could not raise audible alarms. Instead, the data was sent silently to a computer.

"When I discovered they were inhibited a year ago I inquired why, and the explanation I got was that from the OIM (the top Transocean official on the rig) on down, they did not want people woken up at 3:00 a.m. due to false alarms," Williams testified.[6] Williams said that he reported the inhibited alarms to senior subsea supervisor Mark Hay, but Hay was already aware of the situation.

Transocean responded to the allegation with the following statement:

> This is an option on each individual vessel designed to prevent the general alarm from sounding unnecessarily when one of the hundreds of local alarms activates for what could be a minor issue or a non-emergency. Repeated false alarms increase risk and decrease rig safety.[7]

In a later session of the joint hearings, Hay denied approving the bypassed alarm settings. Witnesses agree that the general alarm never sounded that night to warn of dangerously high gas levels on the drilling deck. Alarms were finally triggered only after the gas had ignited and the fire had broken out.

Transocean senior subsea supervisor Mark Hay testifies during the Deepwater Horizon joint investigation hearings in Houston, Texas.

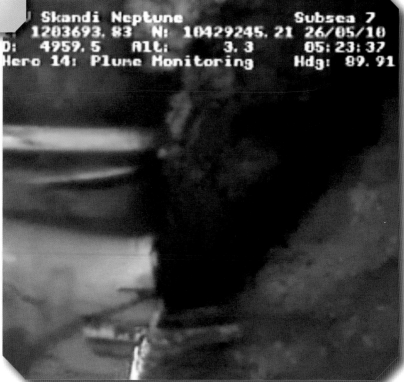

Skandi Neptune   Subsea 7
    1203693.83   N: 10429245.21 26/05/18
D: 4959.5   Alt: 3.3   05:23:37
Hero 14: Plume Monitoring   Hdg: 89.91

Oil spills into the Gulf after the explosion on Deepwater Horizon.

EFFORTS TO STOP
THE OIL LEAK

eanwhile, as investigations deepened
into the cause of the explosion, workers
still needed to address the situation on the ground.
On April 22, 2010, two days after catching fire, the
Deepwater Horizon collapsed and sank. The riser

pipe that connected the well to the rig bent and broke. High-pressure oil began gushing out of the broken riser pipe and the top of the BOP.

This gushing oil was not just an economic loss for BP, which could no longer capture the oil it had been drilling for. It was also a serious environmental threat to sea life in the Gulf of Mexico. It was imperative that the leak be stopped as quickly as possible. The US federal government and BP cooperated in the effort to cap the leak and clean up the spill. BP's chief operating officer Doug Suttles led the company's effort. His counterpart from the federal government was retired US Coast Guard Admiral Thad Allen.

The Worst Oil Spill in US History

Unlike oil tanker spills, in which the volume of the spill is limited to the capacity of the tanker, the Gulf oil spill came directly from the reservoir. The amount of oil in the reservoir was unknown. And the exact amount of oil leaking into the ocean was difficult to determine. It was certain, however, to be more oil than a tanker could ever hold. The environmental damage is expected to be the worst in US history. BP is responsible for the spill, and the company agreed to pick up the bill for the cleanup.

"What is unique about this problem on the ocean floor is that all the capability and capacity to bring to bear on the solution is owned by the private sector. There is a role for government here in terms of oversight and making sure they do what they have promised to do," Admiral Allen explained. "They have the means to do this. We just need to make sure they do it."[1]

MANY FAILED EFFORTS

The oil leak was discovered on April 24. BP immediately sent in a team of experts to cap it. The team, led by BP executive vice president Harry Thierens, deployed remotely controlled submersibles with robotic arms. Robots were used because human divers could not survive the extreme pressure that exists under almost one mile (1.6 km) of water. The robots were able to manipulate

Human Divers Could Not Repair the Well

In August 2007, US Navy diver Daniel Jackson set the record for the deepest dive ever survived by a human: 2,000 feet (609 m). The dive occurred off the coast of La Jolla, California. Jackson wore a hard-shelled suit called the Hard Suit 2000, developed for submarine rescue operations. With its bell helmet, the Hard Suit 2000 looks something like an astronaut's space suit. Its hard shell was essential because pressure at this depth is strong enough to compress a human's lungs. Recreational divers only go as deep as 100 feet (30 m). Divers may go as deep as approximately 350 feet (106 m), but those depths are extremely dangerous.

The Macondo wellhead is 5,000 feet (1,500 m) deep, too deep for even a diver in a hard-shelled suit. The seafloor there is dark even during the daytime because light cannot penetrate through that much water. The temperature never rises above 40 degrees Fahrenheit (4°C). The combination of the pressure, near freezing temperature, and toxic oil and gas gushing from the well would make the survival of a human diver impossible.

controls on the BOP, but the controls did not work as expected. The team would need a new plan to cap the well.

The Cofferdam Containment Dome

On May 7, 2010, BP lowered the giant cofferdam containment dome over the wellhead. The dome stood four stories tall and weighed 100 short tons (91 t). It was made to fit over the leaking wellhead like a suction cup, trapping the oil inside. A pipe would then pump oil to tankers on the surface. The dome was not intended to be a permanent fix, but it was supposed to trap leaking oil until a relief well could be drilled.

"This has never been done in 5,000 feet of water; it is a technology first," BP chief executive officer (CEO) Tony Hayward said. "The pressure and temperatures are very different here, so we cannot be confident that it will work."[2]

As Hayward feared, the cofferdam containment dome did not work. The opening on the top containment became clogged. Oil and gas flowed into the dome so quickly that it began to float. The cofferdam containment dome had failed.

The Top Hat

On May 12, a smaller containment dome dubbed the "top hat" arrived at the well site. At only five feet (1.5 m) tall, less water could fit inside this dome. This design limited the formation of the slush that disabled the larger cofferdam containment dome. Pipes that carried warm water and methanol antifreeze from the surface gave additional protection.

The top hat containment dome was temporarily set aside when BP came up with another tactic, the insertion tube.

The Insertion Tube

On May 15, BP engineers inserted a four-inch (10-cm) tube into the broken riser pipe and began pumping some of the oil to a tanker on the surface. The oil rose up a pipe almost one mile (1.6 km) long to the Discoverer Enterprise drill ship, which transferred it to barges for transport.

The insertion tube did not stop the spill, but it was not expected to. It did prevent some oil from entering Gulf waters. It also bled off some of the pressure from the well. This pressure reduction would make it easier to cap the well.

Two More Failures

On May 28, BP injected heavy drilling mud into the well in a procedure known as top kill. The heavy mud was intended to slow or stop the oil from rising out of the well. On the same day, a junk shot into the BOP was also performed. A junk shot involves shooting junk, such as old golf balls and shredded tires, into the BOP to clog it. This tactic has worked in the past, but never at this depth.

By May 29, it was clear that both tactics had failed. Oil was still flowing into the Gulf.

Another Containment Dome

BP then decided to cut the fractured pipe and attempt to fit a new cap over the freshly cut pipe. By June 3, robot submarines were fitting the new containment dome into place. This dome had valves that were left open initially to prevent the formation of ice crystals. The cap did not immediately stop the flow of oil. Engineers were concerned that suddenly closing the valves would

Stuck Diamond Saw

On June 2, BP engineers ran into a problem as they were trying to prepare the well for capping with a new containment dome. In order to fit the dome, two sections of the broken riser pipe had to be cut off. After one successful cut, a diamond wire saw got stuck in the second pipe and could not be released. A pair of giant shears was substituted. The shears worked, but once the pipe was cut, the flow of oil increased.

BP Chief Operating Officer Doug Suttles speaks in front of a remotely operated underwater vehicle, which assisted in operations at the Deepwater Horizon oil well leak site.

cause the well to blow out lower down. A leak in the subsea well casing would be especially difficult to reach. The valves were initially left open, and some oil still escaped.

A Better Cap

On July 10, the containment dome was removed from the well so that a better cap could be installed. The key to this operation was unfastening the three-inch (7.6-cm) bolts that had attached the riser to the top of the BOP. No one was certain that the remotely operated vehicle (ROV) operators would be able to do this, but the job went smoothly. However, for two days oil flowed unimpeded from the well. By July 12, the installation of the new 150,000-pound (68,000-kg) cap had been tightly bolted into place on the top of the BOP. This cap was supposed to contain the oil completely.

Pressure tests began on July 15, and for the first time, the valves on the containment cap were fully closed. By this point, oil had been flowing into the Gulf of Mexico for 87 days.

Though the flow of oil had finally stopped, engineers did not relax. They were busy testing the pressure of the well. Low pressures would mean that a leak had sprung somewhere in the system.

Pressure Tests

Pressure tests came back with surprisingly low readings. Engineers debated the significance of these readings. The well had spewed oil for three months. Could it finally be losing pressure, or was there a leak somewhere?

Further inspections showed possible methane leaks around the BOP and a seep where oil and methane bubbled up from the seafloor. Experts were

Natural Oil Seeps

Satellite surveys have spotted 600 natural oil seeps in the Gulf of Mexico. Scientists estimate that the total volume of seeped oil in the Gulf equals four times the capacity of the ill-fated *Exxon Valdez* oil tanker, which crashed and spilled in Alaska in 1989.

Oil seeps, unlike human-caused oil spills, cause no significant harm to the environment. Oil from natural seeps is released a little at a time, giving bacteria time to degrade it. The oil never becomes thick enough to coat birds or kill sea turtles, as human-caused oil spills do. The presence of naturally occurring seeps should not be construed to mean that human-caused spills are in any way natural or acceptable.

concerned that this could mean the well casing was cracked somewhere deep below the seafloor.

Pressure was monitored for weeks, and the news was encouraging. Steadily rising pressure indicated that the well casing was intact. The well might soon be capped for good.

STATIC KILL

Static kill, a plan to permanently block the leaking well with heavy mud and concrete, had to wait on the results of the pressure tests. BP and government scientists agreed that a prematurely capped well could result in a subsea blowout. If such a blowout were to occur, it would be virtually impossible to close. Finally, the tests were complete.

On August 3, the site of the spill was crowded with ships and rigs of all descriptions. Transocean rig Discovery Enterprise was there preparing for the static kill procedure. Another rig named Q4000 pumped heavy mud one mile (1.6 km) down the well, forcing the oil down toward the reservoir. One day later the news was good. The pressure of the mud pushing down was equal to the pressure from the oil surging up. The oil leak was finally stopped.

Someone Had Tampered with the BOP

Meanwhile, during attempts to stop the leak, Harry Thierens had discovered something wrong with the BOP. On August 25, Thierens stunned the world with a revelation about the BOP. In testimony before a federal panel in Houston, Thierens said that the BOP had been connected wrong. It would never have worked. A line that should have been attached to the ram was actually connected to a test ram. If connected properly to the ram, it would have been able to cut the pipe in an emergency.

The test ram was meant for use only during pressure tests. It could not have prevented a blowout. According to Thierens, this error would mean that the "test ram would close in an emergency, but it would not be capable of withstanding pressure from below."[3]

A dome was made to be placed on top of the containment box as part of BP's response to the Deepwater Horizon oil spill.

Test rams hold pressure from the top, so they can be used for pressure tests. But they cannot hold against the very real danger of methane rising up from below. This explains why the rig had such trouble with kicks of methane gas. It also explains why the giant bubble of methane was able to erupt from the well, ignite, and destroy the rig.

Thierens's team discovered the faulty design when controls that should have closed valves—shutting off the oil leak—actually operated the ineffectual test ram. The illegal replacement of the BOP's safety rams with test rams made a robotic fix impossible.

The BOP, like the rig itself, was owned by Transocean. Initially, the information about the faulty BOP seemed to shift blame onto Transocean. Then another important fact came to light: the BOP had been altered after it was leased to BP.

Hay testified that he was involved in altering the safety rams on the BOP into test rams in 2004 or 2005. And according to Hay, BP was aware of the conversion. Exactly who else knew about the test rams is uncertain. But the reason the alterations were done was obvious: they saved money. With test rams installed in place of real ones, the rig would not have to stop drilling to run pressure tests. The company saved the time and money it would take to pull up the drill string and insert test equipment into the well. This process had worked fine until there was an emergency.

The BOP Brought to the Surface

On September 7, the BOP from the Macondo well was brought to the surface, and a new one was installed in its place. The original BOP was transported to the US Department of Justice for examination.

Bottom Kill

Relief well drilling was temporarily stopped for the static kill procedure, but it resumed afterward. The relief wells were drilled parallel to the leaking one. But at about 18,000 feet (5,486 m) down, they turned to intersect the original well. Only one relief well was needed, but two were drilled in case one missed its target.

The first relief well was predicted to intersect the leaking well by August 15. But hurricanes delayed the drilling. The relief well intersected the blown-out well on September 17, 2010. That day, the bottom kill procedure began. Concrete was pumped through the relief well and into the leaking one. In just 24 hours, the ruptured well was sealed permanently. This ensured that no pressure surges would bring oil and gas back out of the well.

"It will virtually assure us there's no chance of oil leaking into the environment," Admiral Allen said. "I think we can all breathe a little easier regarding the potential [that] we'll have oil in the Gulf ever again."[4]

A Helix Energy Solutions Q4000 platform gets set to start the static kill operation at the BP Macondo well site in July 2010.

Crude oil is shown in a marsh area in Blind Bay, Louisiana.

Environmental Effects
of the Spill

By the end of August 2010, an estimated 5 million barrels of oil had spilled into the Gulf of Mexico. Approximately 826,800 barrels of oil were skimmed, collected through the insertion pipe, or burned off the surface of the water. Cleanup of the Gulf oil spill cost BP $4 billion, but that figure pales in comparison with the cost to the environment.

A TIPPING POINT

The Gulf oil spill was especially serious because it hit an ecosystem that was already struggling from pollution, development, and fishing pressure. Ecologists are concerned that the Gulf ecosystem could reach a tipping point, in which it will no longer have the resilience to recover from damage.

The long-term nature of the spill made it a bigger threat to the ecosystem, as Louisiana State University oceanography professor James Cowan Jr. explained:

> The longer it [the spill] goes, it's quickly approaching a chronic stressor, which can be much more deleterious. A chronic stressor keeps pushing and pushing the

The Clean Water Act

The Clean Water Act mandates that a company responsible for an oil spill in the United States pay penalties based on the number of barrels of oil spilled. Fines are set at $1,100 per barrel or $4,300 per barrel if the government finds the company guilty of gross negligence.

These fines might be why BP reported during the spill that only 5,000 barrels a day were leaked. However, the publication of underwater video showed large volumes of oil gushing from a broken pipe.

The US Department of the Interior commissioned a study on the amount of oil that had leaked into the Gulf waters. The scientists reported that BP had greatly underestimated the spill. During the height of the crisis, between 35,000 and 65,000 barrels of oil a day flowed into the Gulf.

system until it reaches a tipping point. It may never recover to a state like it was previously.[1]

The Dead Zone

When fertilizer gets washed into a pond, the nutrients cause an overgrowth of algae. Algae produce oxygen by photosynthesis, just as plants do. But, when the algae die, aerobic bacteria decompose them. The aerobic bacteria use up all the dissolved oxygen in the water. Without oxygen, fish and other aquatic organisms suffocate. This process is called eutrophication. It is the reason that many ponds are often green and scummy.

The Gulf of Mexico has the same problem as an overfertilized farm pond, but on a much larger scale. The Mississippi River drains large tracts of farmland, bringing fertilizer runoff, pesticides, and sewage into the waters of the Gulf. This pollution results in a huge dead zone near the Mississippi River Delta, where aerobic bacteria deplete dissolved oxygen. The dead zone in the Gulf usually measures about 6,000 to 7,000 square miles (15,500 to 19,100 sq km). Dead zones have developed along many populated coastlines. There is not enough dissolved oxygen in a dead zone for fish to survive, but jellyfish thrive there. Once large jellyfish populations become established, fish populations tend to decline because jellyfish prey on fish eggs and young fish.

To solve the problem, ecologists advocate reducing manure runoff from factory farms and encourage organic farming.

A DISASTROUS BREEDING SEASON

After the spill, hundreds of thousands of seabirds, jellyfish, and mammals were soaked in oil—most fatally. The Gulf of Mexico is a major flyway for migratory birds, with as many as 25 million passing through in a given day. Seabirds that paused to rest and feed became coated in oil. The birds then ingested the oil as they preened, or cleaned their feathers. Thousands of seabirds were brought to wildlife rescue centers, but many more died unnoticed.

The spill occurred during the worst possible time for the birds—the spring breeding season. The marshes of the Louisiana shoreline are a critical habitat for shorebirds that raise their young there. Migrating birds also stop in the wetlands to rest and feed before continuing on their journeys. Since the spill happened in spring, the oil that washed up into the marshes did not just kill adult birds. Nestlings died too, either from direct oiling or from being fed items contaminated with the poisonous oil.

A Beached Baby Dolphin

On June 24, 41-year-old Christy Travis and her family found an oil-covered baby dolphin struggling on a Florida beach.

"It was so sad. It just broke our hearts," Travis said, recalling how the baby dolphin cried out loud as they tried to help by scraping oil off it with their bare hands. "We had oil all over us."[2]

The Travis family called a wildlife officer, but the baby dolphin died on the way to a rescue center at Gulf World Marine Park. Local resident

Dee Pitman, age 57, was in the crowd that gathered for the three-hour dolphin rescue attempt. Like many coastal residents, she was furious with BP.

"BP doesn't get it," Pitman said. "This is sacred ground to us. We got married on these shores. We baptized our children in this ocean. We entrust the ashes of our loved ones in this ocean."[3]

Endangered Sea Turtles Incinerated

To stop oil from washing onto delicate marshes, BP and the US Coast Guard carried out controlled burns of oil slicks. Out-of-work shrimpers and boat workers did most of the work. The boat captains were hired by BP to collect oil from the surface using floating booms. When enough oil was collected, it was set on fire inside a burn box of fireproof booms.

Endangered Bluefin Tuna Hit Hard

Fish in the northern Gulf of Mexico spawn in the spring. Of special concern is the critically endangered Atlantic population of bluefin tuna. Overfishing has decimated the population of these enormous fish, which can reach 1,500 pounds (680 kg). Stocks are now 10 percent of their former size.

Bluefin tuna return to specific spots on the ocean surface for breeding. Their main spawning zone is very close to the Macondo well. The eggs float near the surface, and the baby tuna swim near the surface after they hatch.

A pelican tries to clean its wings while standing on a rock in the water near Grand Isle, Louisiana.

On June 13, 2010, Mike Ellis, a boat captain working on oil cleanup for BP and the US Coast Guard, announced to the public that BP was incinerating sea turtles during controlled burns. Sea turtles caught inside booms were unable to escape on their own.

National Oceanic and Atmospheric
Administration (NOAA) regulations require crews
to look for turtles before setting the fires. But, Ellis
believes that not all turtle deaths were accidental.

Ellis had been working for a turtle rescue
organization that rushed to free trapped turtles
before the burn boxes were torched. They took the
turtles to rehabilitation centers. The survivors were
later released in cleaner waters. But suddenly, with
no explanation, BP stopped allowing the rescues.
"They ran us out of there and then they shut us
down, they would not let us get back in there,"
Captain Ellis explained. "In the meantime, how
many turtles got caught up and burned?"[4]

Ellis suspects that the turtle incineration was
intentional because BP is liable for up to $50,000
for each endangered animal killed by the spill.
Rescue centers preserve the bodies of endangered
animals they cannot save for later counts. Most of
the oiled turtles were Kemp's Ridley sea turtles, an
endangered species.

In the wake of a lawsuit, BP spokesman Mark
Proegler said that crews are instructed to look for
turtles before oil is burned. They are not to start
fires if one is spotted. The idea that turtles may have

been burned is "appalling," Proegler said. "That would never be done intentionally. I can't say for sure we've never burned any, but every effort is taken to avoid that."[5]

THE DISPERSANT CONTROVERSY

Oil normally floats on water, but much of the oil from the Gulf spill formed into giant undersea plumes. These oil plumes did not rise to the surface. It is possible that the plumes formed because of the use of dispersants. Dispersants are chemicals that emulsify oil. They break it down into small droplets. In an attempt to stop oil from reaching beaches, BP used airplanes to spray dispersants over the oil slick. Even more dispersants were released underwater.

The dispersants themselves are known to be toxic. However, because of the seriousness of the oil spill, the Environmental Protection Agency (EPA) deemed dispersants worth the risk. Oil contamination of the shoreline would destroy fisheries. The dispersants will have long-term effects on the ecology of the Gulf of Mexico, but the severity and the exact nature of these effects remain unknown.

"It's a whole new ball game," said Ted Van Vleet, a professor of chemical oceanography in the college

of Marine Science at the University
of South Florida. "People are totally
unsure as to how it is going to affect
the ecosystems."[6]

DISPERSED OIL IS HIDDEN, NOT GONE

Approximately one month
after the leak was capped, good
news began coming in from coastal
communities. Although some tar
balls—blobs of solidified tar that
result from oil spills—continued to
wash up, beaches were cleaner than
expected. On August 27, 2010,
NOAA reopened 4,281 square
miles (11,087 sq km) of Gulf waters
to recreational and commercial
fishing. People celebrated,
marveling at how the oil seemed to
have evaporated.

Dr. Samantha Joye was one of the
principal investigators on a NOAA
study of the deepwater impacts of the
spill. She knew that the oil was not

Threatened and Endangered Species of the Gulf of Mexico

- Sperm whales
- Leatherback sea turtles
- Hawksbill sea turtles
- Green sea turtles
- Loggerhead sea turtles
- Kemp's Ridley sea turtles
- Smalltooth sawfish
- Gulf sturgeon
- Elkhorn coral
- Staghorn coral

really gone. Its presence was just not obvious. Joye explained:

> While some of the oil has most certainly evaporated, much of it was dispersed and this oil is still floating around, invisible to our eyes, within the ocean's water column. Some of the oil has probably sedimented to the seafloor, where it is also invisible to our eyes. The fact that this oil is "invisible" makes it no less of a danger to the Gulf's fragile ecosystems. Quite the contrary, the danger is real and the danger is much more difficult to quantify, track and assess.[7]

Joye's study was conducted from the research ship *Pelican* during the summer of 2010. As marine scientists tracked the movement of oil and gas through the food web, they made a startling discovery. Huge plumes of undersea oil were hanging suspended in the water of the Gulf of Mexico. The main plume was 30 miles (48 km) long by seven miles (11 km) wide. And several more had been spotted. Tests confirmed that the plumes originated at the Macondo well.

Naturally occurring microbes will eventually break down these plumes. The problem is that oil-eating microbes are aerobic. This means they can use up dissolved oxygen in oily water. Fish and other

The Deepest Spill Ever

People may imagine that a deepwater oil spill falls into a dark, desolate place, bereft of all life. But in fact, deep-sea coral reefs host diverse communities of fish, jellyfish, sharks, crabs, and shrimp. This is the first deep-sea oil spill, so the damage to the ecosystem is difficult to predict. At the seafloor, there is no weathering from tides or wind, so oil will probably take longer to break down than it would on the surface.

marine organisms that swim into a plume may not get enough oxygen through their gills. They would also be exposed to toxic petroleum products, including benzene, toluene, and xylene. At high doses these chemicals can kill. In dilute amounts, they stunt growth and slow or stop reproduction of marine life. In either case, the plumes are going to be a long-term danger to life in the Gulf.

Oil coats the waters of the Gulf of Mexico in April 2010.

Cleanup workers are exposed to toxins in the oil.

THE IMPACT ON HUMAN HEALTH

il is toxic, whether it is ingested, inhaled, or absorbed through the skin. Although there have been many oil spills, few studies have followed the health of area residents. Coastal residents may face risks, but little is known about the effects of low-dose, long-term exposure. Research usually focuses on cleanup workers because they face the highest risk. Cleanup workers inhale petroleum fumes for prolonged periods. They also frequently get oil on their skin.

In 2002, the oil tanker *Prestige* was wrecked in a storm off the coast of Spain. A massive oil spill was released when the tanker broke up and sank. It took Spanish workers more than one year to clean their beaches. A study of the cleanup workers revealed that many suffered from respiratory symptoms and permanent airway injuries, probably from inhaling petroleum fumes.

Of even greater concern were reports of chromosomal damage in the Spanish workers' white blood cells. This was worrisome because mutations are associated with an increased risk of cancer. Exposure to a carcinogen, a substance that causes cancer, does not necessarily lead to cancer. It takes multiple mutations to cause cancer, so a single exposure to a carcinogen poses little risk. This

DNA, Mutations, and Cancer

DNA is a long molecule that coils up to form the chromosomes that carry genetic information. DNA can be damaged, or mutated, by exposure to certain chemicals, including some found in oil. Chemicals that can damage DNA are called mutagens. Many carcinogens (substances that cause cancer) are mutagenic. DNA has some ability to repair itself, but mutations that are not repaired can mean an increased risk of cancer.

is why smokers usually get cancer decades—instead of days—after they begin smoking.

The Spanish workers had long-term exposure to toxins because their cleanup operation took many months. Fortunately, follow-up testing showed that their DNA damage repaired itself over time.

CANCER RISK IN GULF COAST COMMUNITIES

The biggest public health concern about the Gulf oil spill is whether it will boost cancer rates in coastal communities. Higher cancer rates are a real possibility because crude oil contains benzene and polycyclic aromatic hydrocarbons (PAHs). Both of these chemicals are carcinogens. PAHs are also toxic to the brain and central nervous system.

The Symptoms of Oil Toxicity

Workers cleaning up an oil spill may suffer from some or all of these symptoms:
- coughs and other respiratory symptoms
- dizziness
- headaches
- nausea
- rashes
- stinging eyes

Benzene and PAHs lend oil its petroleum odor, so someone who catches a whiff of oil just inhaled a mixture of carcinogens. That is less alarming than it may sound because of the short duration of the exposure. However, the Gulf spill lasted for months, and these compounds are volatile. They evaporated easily from surface oil slicks, became airborne,

and were carried inland by winds.
Louisiana and Florida residents were
certainly exposed to low levels of
benzene and PAHs, throughout the
summer of 2010.

Weathered oil is less dangerous
than freshly spilled oil because
volatile compounds, such as benzene
and PAHs, have already evaporated
off. For Gulf cleanup workers this
meant that the people on boats
skimming up fresh oil sometimes
became ill, but volunteers cleaning
up tar balls on the beach were
fairly safe.

DISPERSANTS

Dispersants are chemicals made
specifically for use after an oil spill.
Two dispersants used after the Gulf
spill are versions of a product called
Corexit. Despite the name, which
is pronounced like "corrects it,"
Corexit does not really correct the problem. The
dispersant does not take oil out of the water. And

The Dangers of Dispersants

Corexit is a mixture of solvents and detergent-like surfactants. Its exact composition, however, is an industry secret. According to a Center for Disease Control (CDC) report, the solvents are low-toxicity, and the product is biodegradable. However, a main ingredient in Corexit is the organic solvent 2-butoxy-ethanol. The same CDC report goes on to warn that excessive exposure to 2-butoxyethanol may cause damage to the central nervous system. Symptoms of exposure may include depression, nausea, vomiting, and anesthetic or narcotic effects. It may also damage red blood cells, the kidneys, or the liver.

dispersed oil cannot be skimmed. Dispersants break oil up into small droplets, allowing microbes to more easily break it down.

Most applications of Corexit occurred at sea, and humans were not exposed greatly. Dispersants are made to sink when they contact oil, which also helps minimize human exposure. However, on some occasions dispersants blew back on shore, causing illness in coastal residents.

This happened to Barbara and Warren Schebler of Homosassa, Florida. They had no idea that their backyard pool was contaminated with dispersants. They first noticed the problem when they both got rashes in May. After swimming in the family pool, Warren got severe diarrhea and passed strange, dark colored urine. The Scheblers suspected a water problem and sent samples to a lab for testing. Results revealed 50.3 ppm (parts per million) 2-butoxyethanol, a chemical in Corexit.

"At night we would hear very low aircraft, including helicopters," Barbara recalled. "We figured they were just heading to help out in the Gulf. The prevailing winds from the Gulf are easterly—and when they spray, it is airborne—and we are right in the path of those winds."[1]

Is Gulf Seafood Safe to Eat?

The Food and Drug Administration (FDA) has cleared Gulf seafood as safe. But some scientists are not convinced. Gina Solomon is a medical doctor and public health expert in the department of medicine at the University of California at San Francisco. She coauthored a controversial report published in August 2010 in the *Journal of the American Medical Association*. The report declared that Gulf shrimp, oysters, and crabs are likely to be contaminated by PAHs.

Vicki Seyfert-Margolis of the FDA disagreed, stating that the FDA does not believe PAH contamination is a problem. The FDA has a mussel watch program that regularly tests Gulf seafood. Before an area of the Gulf is opened for fishing, seafood from that spot must pass stringent tests for safety.

The problem is that plumes of oil drift about, and animals move as well. According to Ronald Kendall, chairman of Texas Tech University's Department of Environmental Toxicology:

Dispersants Are More Toxic When Combined with Oil

Laboratory tests by the Environmental Protection Agency (EPA) determined that dispersants combined with oil were more toxic than dispersants alone. Dispersants were used only where oil was present.

We must continue to monitor this very closely. Shellfish may be clear now, but in two months maybe not, depending on how the oil moves. You can't just test once and stop. There's a lot of oil in the Gulf, and we don't know where it all is.[2]

Biological Magnification

Biological magnification is the process by which a toxin becomes more concentrated as it moves up the food chain. The process begins when oil-eating microbes absorb traces of mercury naturally found in oil. The microbes can digest the oil but not the mercury. Mercury is a heavy metal, and it cannot be broken down. A minuscule amount is stored in each tiny cell.

The microbes are prey for other tiny organisms, which are in turn eaten by larger ones. Each predator must eat many prey animals to survive, so predators accumulate the toxins stored in the bodies of each prey animal. The mercury moves into small fish, which are eaten by successively larger ones. The poison becomes more concentrated at each step until the largest and oldest fish carry dangerous doses of mercury.

Humans are at the top of this food chain. People can get mercury poisoning from eating large amounts of fish, especially if they prefer predatory species, such as tuna or orange roughy. Other fish species that are too high in mercury for safe consumption include king mackerel, shark, marlin, swordfish, tilefish, and bigeye tuna.

Solomon has another concern: The spill may have contaminated the entire Gulf food chain with mercury. Mercury is a natural component of oil, and the spill has distributed it widely. Most people are exposed to mercury primarily through consuming contaminated fish. Mercury poisoning causes disabilities in babies when they are exposed to high levels in the womb. At lower levels, mercury damages the brain, impairing cognition, memory, and attention. Children are more sensitive to mercury than adults, so doctors warn pregnant women and mothers of young children to limit the amount of fish they eat. Solomon expects to hear more such warnings about Gulf seafood.

"Several years from now the concentration [of mercury] will go up in fish at the top of the food chain—tuna, mackerel, swordfish," Solomon said.[3]

MORE STUDIES ARE NEEDED

Compounds in oil are toxic. People who work around petroleum fumes face an increased risk of cancer. So what risk does the public face from the Gulf oil spill? James Giordano is director of the Center for Neurotechnology Studies at the Potomac Institute for Policy Studies in Arlington, Virginia. According to Giordano:

> There is overwhelming evidence that many of the compounds found in crude oil are dangerous. It will be important to have a regional and national public health effort to assess the health impact.[4]

Officials at the National Institutes of Health (NIH) agreed. In August 2010, the NIH announced a $10 million long-term health study of 20,000 Gulf workers and residents. The research focuses on the effect of oil exposure on the health of cleanup workers and volunteers. ⌐

Despite health concerns, some areas of the Gulf were still open to fishermen after August 27.

Out-of-work fishermen wait to hear from a BP company representative of the plan to have fishermen help clean up the oil spill in the Gulf of Mexico.

FINANCIAL LOSSES AND LITIGATION

From the oil industry to fishing to tourism, it seemed that no business had gone unaffected by the Gulf spill. Financially, the impact of the Gulf spill would extend far beyond what anyone had imagined.

DEEPWATER DRILLING IS HALTED

Shortly after the spill, in May 2010 US President Barack Obama called for a temporary halt on deepwater drilling. President Obama cited safety concerns as the reason for this controversial decision. As evidence of safety violations on Deepwater Horizon came to light, it seemed that safety standards on other oil rigs may need to be addressed to ensure against another disaster.

An estimated 11,000 jobs were temporarily affected by the ban, which halted activity on 33 rigs. The moratorium was overturned in court, but the Obama administration immediately issued a revised version based on the rig's safety equipment rather than on water depth.

FISHING WATERS CONTAMINATED

Fishermen and shrimpers also lost income in the immediate aftermath of the spill. Contaminated areas of the Gulf were closed to fishing. Fishermen's jobs were put

The Gulf Needs a Good Lawyer

In 2009, BP had to file a spill cleanup plan before it was cleared for exploratory drilling. In their plan, the company said that in the event of a spill it could skim up to 20 million gallons (76 million l) of oil per day. During the Gulf spill, BP only reclaimed 2 percent of that amount.

In June 2010, the environmental law firm Earthjustice filed a lawsuit against the US Minerals Management Service. This is the agency that approved BP's cleanup plan. An Earthjustice victory would force BP to come up with a more realistic cleanup plan before doing any more exploratory drilling.

on hold until the waters were safe. BP promised compensation for lost income, and it could not come fast enough. Boat owners were not able to pay their bills, and they were threatened with foreclosure. Their entire livelihoods were at stake. Although BP hired some fishing boat captains to help clean up the spill, many were left idle.

"It's a weird situation here, and it's a sad situation," said fisherman Peter Gerica of New Orleans. "Most of these guys have been sitting for 90 to 100 days, not having a dime."[1]

Jobs Lost

Because of the contaminated water, tourists

Vessels of Opportunity

In a program called Vessels of Opportunity, BP hired out-of-work fishing boat captains at a rate of $1,200 per day to clean up spilled oil. Many small boats were needed to lay floating booms to keep oil off of beaches and wetlands. Others would assist in skimming or controlled burns. "We are trying to put money back in your community; that is why we are here," said BP community outreach organizer David Kinnaird to a meeting of fishing boat captains.[2]

The 1,900 contracts issued to boat captains were intended to diminish anger at BP. But some say the Vessels of Opportunity program turned into a scandal. Biloxi boat captain Tom Becker claims that in his Mississippi harbor, 90 percent of the contracts went to pleasure boats owned by doctors, lawyers, and other wealthy professionals.

"Every day I see the boat trailers fill the parking lot as the pleasure boats get their assignments for the day while the commercial fleet sits idle. This is like stealing. These jokers are taking money away from those who are trying to feed their families," Becker said.[3]

canceled reservations at Gulf Coast resorts. Oil was washing up on many beaches. And although many more beaches were unaffected by the oil spill, tourists preferred to stay away.

As a result, sportfishing operations, hotels, and restaurants all languished. Deckhands, busboys, cooks, and other employees of these industries were out of work. Businesses those employees once patronized were hurt as well. In all, an estimated 17,000 jobs in the Gulf Coast region were lost due to the spill. The wave of hardship reached as far as Boston, Massachusetts, where a restaurant owner sued because his seafood supply had been cut off.

President Obama made five trips to the Gulf Coast during the summer following the spill. In an attempt to encourage tourists to return, the president and his family were televised swimming at a clean Florida beach and eating locally caught fish.

BP's Compensation Fund

In June 2010, BP succumbed to White House pressure and set up a $20 billion compensation fund for Gulf Coast residents and business owners. Although this is a significant sum, it may not be sufficient to pay all the claims.

The claims process was especially frustrating for fishermen, who could not document losses because their incomes varied from day to day. The fund ended up paying each of them $5,000 a month. But most fishermen would have earned $10,000 to $40,000 a month on the water. Even with earnings like these, most fishermen are not wealthy. Fishing seasons are only a few months long, and payments on fishing boats are quite high. One lost season can make the difference between success and foreclosure.

The Oil Pollution Act of 1990

The Oil Pollution Act sets a cap on the economic damages that oil companies must pay in the event of a spill. The cap is set at $75 million, which is far less than the cost of a major spill. In June 2010, Democrats backed legislation to raise the cap to $10 billion. But Republicans blocked the attempt to raise the cap. US Coast Guard cleanup operations in the Gulf were funded by US taxpayers.

WHO IS ENTITLED TO COMPENSATION?

People who were directly impacted by the spill were sure to be compensated, but what about indirect impacts, such as a bar that lost money when unemployed fishermen stopped coming in?

Those applying for compensation had to prove that their losses were directly due to the spill. Compensation fund administrator Kenneth Feinberg encouraged all victims to apply for compensation.

With many Gulf beaches closed during the summer of 2010, many businesses that rely on tourism suffered.

Feinberg promised deals at least as good as they would get in court.

Stephen J. Herman is the liaison between plaintiffs' lawyers and New Orleans judge Carl Barbier. According to Herman, BP will pay indirect claims, but not for long. "In the short term they might, for PR purposes," Herman said. "But in the long run they won't, because it would bankrupt them."[4]

Looking for Payback

For many victims of the oil spill, lawsuits seemed to be the only solution. In April, a coalition of Louisiana shrimpers filed the first class-action lawsuit against BP, Transocean, and Halliburton. Groups of restaurant owners, real-estate brokers, BP shareholders, and coastal residents quickly followed suit. Environmental organizations even filed lawsuits on behalf of oil-soaked birds and other wildlife. Lawyers flocked to the Gulf Coast, and their advertisements popped up everywhere—even on roadside billboards. By August 2010, 300 suits had been filed. A federal panel decided that US District Judge Carl Barbier would hear most of the cases in New Orleans.

Big court cases such as these often drag on for years, so most of them were not yet resolved by the end of 2010. Judge Barbier was expected to forge a broad settlement that would settle many claims simultaneously. As angry as most of the plaintiffs are with BP, they do agree on one thing: they do not want to see the company driven out of business. In order to pay its debts, BP will need to remain profitable for years to come.

Kenneth R. Feinberg, administrator of BP's compensation fund, speaks in Washington in July 2010.

Steve Barrileaux, a psychologist with the Gulf Coast Mental Health Center, discusses increased levels of mental health issues related to the Gulf oil spill.

A COMMUNITY
UNDER STRESS

The consequences of an oil spill go beyond concerns about health and the environment. There is also a considerable psychological toll to the residents of affected communities. People grieve the damage done, and they worry about the future. Uncertainty creates stress, which may cause people to become violent or act out toward one another.

In the aftermath of an oil spill, strangers stream into small towns to organize the response. A few local people land lucrative jobs helping with the cleanup. But many others lose their jobs.

"Fragmented families, failed marriages, community residents who no longer speak to each other or collaborate in community activities," says social worker Lawrence Palinkas. "It's all part of the strong emotions generated by the disaster—including resentments over friends and family members who profited from it by working in the cleanup."[1]

Disasters in the Gulf

At the time of the oil spill, the Gulf Coast community was still recovering from the devastation caused by Hurricane Katrina, which struck the area in 2005. About 20 percent of New Orleans residents

Oil Remains from the *Exxon Valdez* Spill

The Prince William Sound, on the south coast of Alaska, was the site of the *Exxon Valdez* oil spill in 1989. Until the Gulf oil spill, the *Exxon Valdez* spill was the worst in US history. Today, the area looks as though it has recovered. The water looks clear, and birds forage along its shores. But 21,000 gallons (6,400 l) of oil still remain, trapped under rocks and sediments. There was once an abundant herring fishery in the area, but now the herring are gone. The oil is degrading at a rate of 0 to 4 percent per year. It will take a century for the ecosystem to fully recover.

were unable to evacuate. Waters flooded buildings while looters ran rampant. It took days for the government to send emergency supplies of food and water. Survivors were traumatized and many lost faith in the government's ability to handle a crisis.

When the Gulf oil spill happened, many Louisiana residents were unable to overcome yet another horrible disaster in their community. New Orleans was not even finished rebuilding from Hurricane Katrina. In some neighborhoods, storm-flooded houses still stand, abandoned and molding. The oil spill plunged a recovering community right into another disaster.

"A lot of the issues around

The *Exxon Valdez* Spill

On March 24, 1989, the oil tanker *Exxon Valdez* struck a reef off Prince William Sound in Alaska. It spilled 11 million gallons (42 million l) of oil. Much of what is known about the psychological effects of oil spills comes from studies carried out after this event.

After the *Exxon Valdez* spill, social work professor Lawrence Palinkas of the University of California studied 22 affected communities. He documented marked increases in drinking, drug use, and fighting—all of which are measures of community stress. Alaskans who were directly affected by the spill, such as cleanup workers or fishermen, were much more likely to suffer from PTSD, anxiety disorders, and depression than those who had no contact with oil. Even children were stressed, as measured by increases in bed-wetting, fighting with siblings, and separation anxiety. Visits to local mental health centers increased sharply as well.

Katrina were about mistrust, and we're also seeing a lot of mistrust of government now," said psychologist Nancy Adler, who studied the mental health effects of the Gulf oil spill.[2]

BLOCKED ACCESS TO THE SPILL ZONE

That mistrust intensified during the cleanup process. BP was reluctant to show the public what was going on in the water. They prevented reporters from viewing the area and taking photos.

Throughout the spill, BP used hired security guards to keep observers out of the spill zone. In early July, the US Coast Guard announced that it was now a felony offense for reporters to approach closer than 65 feet (20 m) to any cleanup vessel or boom. The official reason given was safety. According to a Coast Guard press release, the safety zone protected the response effort. It prevented accidental damage to the environment and the oil containment booms being used for cleanup.

But the rule also prevented journalists from getting photographs of oil-soaked birds perched on the floating booms. Even the airspace over the oil slick was restricted, so private planes could not tour the area. Only a few journalists chosen by BP were allowed to film parts of the slick from the air. This secrecy increased the feelings of anger and powerlessness among Gulf Coast residents.

"If we can't show what is happening, warts and all, no one will see what's happening," objected CNN anchorman Anderson Cooper. "And that makes it very easy to hide failure and hide incompetence and makes it very hard to highlight the hard work of cleanup crews and the Coast Guard. We are not the enemy here."[3]

BLAMING TONY HAYWARD

CEO Tony Hayward was the public face of BP during the spill and its cleanup. Many people were angry with BP for having caused the disaster. Some did not feel that BP was taking full responsibility for the accident and its cleanup, which was not happening quickly enough for many people in communities directly affected by the disaster.

Children in the Spill Zone

Some Gulf Coast kids are suffering from unexplained rashes and breathing problems, possibly from exposure to oil or dispersants. July 2010 surveys of parents in the hardest hit areas revealed that one-third of their children were showing psychological symptoms as well. The children's symptoms included nightmares, bickering with playmates, insomnia, nervousness, and anxiety.

Many people blamed Hayward for BP's failures during the spill.

To make things worse, on May 31 Hayward bungled an apology to the people of Louisiana. "The first thing to say is I'm sorry," Hayward said, when asked what he would say to locals whose livelihoods have been affected by the spill. "We're sorry for the massive disruption it's caused their lives. There's no one who wants this over more than I do. I would like my life back."[4]

Christopher Jones, whose brother Gordon was one of the 11 men killed in the accident, responded to Hayward's comment on June 8 during his testimony in Washington DC.

"I want to take this opportunity to address recent remarks made by Tony Hayward, CEO of BP. In particular, he publicly stated he wants his life back. Well, Mr. Hayward, I want my brother's life back," said Jones.[5]

Hayward posted a sincere apology for his statement on his Web site. But his flippant comment had already angered many people suffering in the Gulf. During an anti-BP street demonstration in New Orleans, one unidentified protestor was televised saying, "I'm filled with anxiety every night,

Anderson Cooper and other reporters take a tour of areas affected by the oil spill that are open to the press with Louisiana Governor Bobby Jindal on May 26, 2010, in Blind Bay, Louisiana.

and I hope that the BP executives feel the same way. Unfortunately I doubt that they do."[6]

Hayward did not appear to be filled with anxiety on June 19, when the press spotted him enjoying himself at a yacht race. Meanwhile, back in Louisiana, crews were working around the clock to stop oil from reaching the marshes. The incident highlighted inequities between the upper and lower classes. It also added to the perception that oil executives were merely inconvenienced by a spill that devastated the working class.

On July 27, Hayward yielded to pressure and resigned. Despite the tragedy that occurred on his watch, he still received an $18.5 million severance package from BP.

HELPING COMMUNITIES OVERCOME ANGER

After a disaster, mental health workers train community leaders to organize support groups. People in groups are often more resilient to stress because they can support each other. Volunteers with community outreach programs may even knock on doors to make contact with homebound or isolated citizens.

Counseling centers need to be open to provide a sympathetic ear and to connect people with aid programs. "Let them know what's available to them," Adler says. "Let them know where they can go and who they can talk to for help."[7]

Some counselors may even encourage people to bring attention to the problem through activism. This brings people together and allows them to use their anger in a positive way.

Beyond Petroleum

The Gulf oil spill brought to light some of the real dangers of oil drilling. For some, this accident was evidence that the United States should transition away from petroleum and toward renewable energy.

The transition will not be easy because society is dependent upon oil for its very survival. Fossil fuels are used to make the fertilizers that grow crops, and they run the tractors that plow those same fields. They are even used as raw materials for plastics and pharmaceutical drugs.

Oil reserves that are easy to reach are mostly depleted, so offshore drilling will probably continue. Better enforcement of safety regulations is needed. But as long as there is drilling, there is a chance for another spill.

Greenpeace members hold a protest in Washington on May 5, 2010, to protest the oil spill in the Gulf.

TIMELINE

March 20, 2010	April 20, 2010	April 21, 2010
An accident damages the annular seal on Deepwater Horizon's blowout preventer (BOP).	Deepwater Horizon explodes at 10:00 p.m. Eleven people die. The US Coast Guard launches rescue.	Crew members on lifeboats arrive on shore at 3:00 p.m.

April 25, 2010	April 26, 2010	April 27, 2010
The oil leak is estimated at 1,000 barrels a day; dispersants are applied.	Submersible robots are deployed but they fail to activate the BOP. Containment booms are placed at the spill site.	The joint investigation into the accident begins.

April 22, 2010	April 23, 2010	April 24, 2010
Deepwater Horizon sinks.	The US Coast Guard suspends the search for survivors.	Oil is discovered leaking from the Macondo Prospect well, and robots are deployed.

April 28, 2010	April 30, 2010	May 1, 2010
Oil leak estimates are revised to 5,000 barrels a day. Controlled burns begin.	Oil reaches land and contaminates bayous.	Admiral Thad Allen is named point person for the response.

TIMELINE

May 7, 2010	May 12, 2010	May 15, 2010
The cofferdam containment dome is put in place over the wellhead.	The top hat containment dome replaces the failed cofferdam.	A tube is inserted into the broken pipe on the seafloor to pump some oil to a tanker on the surface.

July 15, 2010	August 3, 2010	August 25, 2010
The valves on the containment cap are fully closed; oil stops leaking into the Gulf.	Static kill permanently blocks the leaking well with heavy mud and concrete.	BP's Harry Thierens reveals that the BOP was faulty.

May 28, 2010

BP injects heavy drilling mud into the well in a procedure known as top kill and performs a junk shot into the BOP. Both efforts fail.

June 3, 2010

A new containment dome is installed.

July 12, 2010

Installation of a new 150,000-pound (68,000-kg) cap is complete.

September 7, 2010

The BOP is brought to the surface for examination.

September 17, 2010

The bottom kill procedure plugs the leaking well.

Essential Facts

Date of Event

April 20, 2010

Place of Event

Gulf of Mexico

Key Players

* BP
* Transocean
* Halliburton
* US Coast Guard
* Bureau of Ocean Energy Management, Regulation and Enforcement
* US Congress
* Deepwater Horizon Crew
* Gulf Coast residents and workers

Highlights of Event

* On the morning of the accident, BP representative Donald Vidrine directed the crew to replace drilling mud with seawater before capping the well. This was risky, but it would speed up the job. The Transocean crew objected but followed orders.

* At around 10:00 p.m. on April 20, 2010, the Macondo well in the Gulf of Mexico blew out, igniting a firestorm that killed 11 people. The accident occurred because a large volume of methane rose up out of the well and ignited.

- Crew members who survived the explosion were held on lifeboats for 15 hours and were required to sign waivers before they were allowed to rest or see family members.

- Beginning in May 2010, the US Coast Guard and the Bureau of Ocean Energy Management, Regulation and Enforcement held joint hearings to investigate the accident. Investigations revealed that the alarm, which could have warned the crew of gas on the deck, was deliberately bypassed. Throughout the investigation, companies tried to shift blame onto each other.

- Hundreds of thousands of marine mammals, birds, fish, and sea turtles died in the spill. Some coastal residents have been sickened by exposure to oil or dispersants. Dispersants caused large plumes of oil to float beneath the surface, poisoning marine life.

- Several containment domes and caps were deployed in an attempt to stop the leak. All failed, until mid-July when a new 150,000-pound (68,000-kg) cap was installed. Valves were slowly closed over a period of days, and the oil leak was stopped.

Quote

"I did not appreciate what I considered to be a ridiculous spectacle during the congressional hearings into this matter. You had executives of BP and Transocean and Halliburton falling over each other to point the finger of blame at somebody else."—*President Barack Obama*

"If we can't show what is happening, warts and all, no one will see what's happening. And that makes it very easy to hide failure and hide incompetence and makes it very hard to highlight the hard work of cleanup crews and the Coast Guard. We are not the enemy here."—*CNN anchorman Anderson Cooper*

GLOSSARY

assess
To evaluate or estimate the extent or significance of something.

carcinogen
A substance that causes cancer.

chronic
Long lasting, characterized by extended periods of suffering.

cognition
Thinking, processing information.

construed
Interpreted, assigned a meaning to.

contaminated
Polluted, impure.

conversion
Transformation, changing from one purpose to another.

deleterious
Harmful to living things.

ecosystem
A system formed by the interaction of living organisms with their environment.

hydraulic
A type of machine moved by water or oil forced through pipes by pumps.

incinerated
Burned to ashes.

ineffectual
Futile, producing no result or effect.

ingested
Consumed, eaten.

mutation
>A change in the structure or base sequence of DNA, the molecule that encodes heritable information.

negligence
>Carelessness, irresponsibility.

prematurely
>Occurring too soon, before the proper time.

psychological
>Having to do with the mind and emotions.

quantify
>To express as a number or quantity.

rehabilitation
>Caring for wounded or orphaned animals and then returning them to the wild.

reprisal
>Retaliatory action or punishment.

ruptured
>Torn or broken open, burst.

stressor
>A man-made factor that damages an ecosystem, an agent that causes stress.

traumatic
>Relating to a psychological or emotional shock, usually due to an upsetting experience.

valve
>A device in pipes that regulates the flow of liquid by opening and closing.

waiver
>A legal document agreeing to hold a person or company blameless in case of accident, injury, or financial loss.

ADDITIONAL RESOURCES

SELECTED BIBLIOGRAPHY

"Animals Hurt by Gulf Oil Spill." *Cbsnews*. CBSInteractive, 16 May 2010. Web.

"Blowout: The Deepwater Horizon Disaster." *Cbsnews.com*. CBS News, 60 Minutes, n.d. Web.

Carroll, Joe, and Laurel Brubaker Calkins. "BP Pressured Rig Worker to Hurry Before Disaster, Father Says." *Bloomberg.com*. Bloomberg, 27 May 2010. Web.

"Is BP burning endangered sea turtles alive with oil from spill?" *News.gather.com*. Gather News Channel, 20 Jun 2010. Web.

Joye, Samantha. "Deepwater Horizon, Gulf of Mexico, Oil Spill Research." *Gulfblog.uga.edu*. Gulf Oil Blog, UGA Department of Marine Sciences, 5 Sep 2010. Web.

FURTHER READINGS

Berger, Melvin, and Paul Mirocha. *Oil Spill!* New York: Harper Collins, 1994. Print.

Bushell, Sharon, and Stan Jones. *The Spill: Personal Stories from the Exxon Valdez Disaster*. Kenmore, WA: Epicenter, 2009. Print.

Leacock, Elspeth. *The Exxon Valdez Oil Spill*. New York: Facts on File, 2005. Print.

Ott, Riki, and John Perkins. *Not One Drop: Betrayal and Courage in the Wake of the Exxon Valdez Oil Spill*. White River Junction, VT: Chelsea Green, 2008. Print.

Parks, Peggy J. *Oil Spills*. San Diego: KidHaven, 2005. Print.

Web Links

To learn more about the Gulf of Mexico oil spill, visit
ABDO Publishing Company online at **www.abdopublishing.com**.
Web sites about the Gulf of Mexico oil spill are featured on our
Book Links page. These links are routinely monitored and updated
to provide the most current information available.

Places to Visit

Alaska Sealife Center
301 Railway Avenue, Seward, AK 99664
888-378-2525
www.alaskasealife.org
Research, rehabilitation, education, and exhibits are presented at
the center.

East Texas Oil Museum
1100 Broadway Boulevard, Kilgore, TX 75662
903-983-8295
www.easttexasoilmuseum.com
Authentic re-creation of oil discovery and production in the early
1930s are on display.

Sea Center Texas
300 Medical Drive, Lake Jackson, TX 77566
979-292-0100
www.tpwd.state.tx.us/spdest/visitorcenters/seacenter
Visitors view large Gulf of Mexico marine animals as well as a one-
of-a-kind marine fish hatchery.

Source Notes

Chapter 1. Catastrophe on the Deepwater Horizon
   1. "Blowout: The Deepwater Horizon Disaster." *Cbsnews.com.* CBS News, 16 May 2010. Web. 20 Sep 2010.
   2. Ibid.
   3. Ibid.
   4. Ibid.
   5. Douglas A. Blackmon, Vanessa O'Connell, Alexandra Berzon, and Ana Campoy. "There Was 'Nobody in Charge.'" *Wall Street Journal.* Dow Jones & Company, Inc., 27 May 2010. Web. 21 Sep 2010.
   6. Ibid.
   7. Ibid.
   8. "Blowout: The Deepwater Horizon Disaster." *Cbsnews.com.* CBS News, 16 May 2010. Web. 20 Sep 2010.
   9. Ibid.

Chapter 2. A Long, Slow Rescue
   1. "Blowout: The Deepwater Horizon Disaster." *Cbsnews.com.* CBS News, 16 May 2010. Web. 20 Sep 2010.
   2. Douglas A. Blackmon, Vanessa O'Connell, Alexandra Berzon, and Ana Campoy. "There Was 'Nobody in Charge.'" *Wall Street Journal.* Dow Jones & Company, Inc., 27 May 2010. Web. 21 Sep 2010.
   3. Joseph Shapiro. "Rig Survivors Felt Coerced To Sign Waivers." *NPR: National Public Radio.* NPR, 6 May 2010. Web. 21 Sep 2010.

Chapter 3. Deepwater Drilling
   1. "Blowout: The Deepwater Horizon Disaster." *Cbsnews.com.* CBS News, 16 May 2010. Web. 20 Sep 2010.
   2. Ibid.

Chapter 4. Risking Lives for Profit

1. Russell Gold. "Oil-Rig Crew Argued Over Drilling Plan Before Blast." *Wall Street Journal*. Dow Jones & Company, Inc., 15 May 2010. Web. 21 Sep 2010.

2. Miguel Bustillo. "Heated Argument on Rig Hours Before Blast." *Wall Street Journal*. Dow Jones & Company, Inc., 27 May 2010. Web. 21 Sep 2010.

3. Ibid.

4. Caren Bohan, and Steve Gorman. "Obama Slams Oil Companies for Spill Blame Game." *Reuters.com*. Thomson Reuters, 14 May 2010. Web. 21 Sep 2010.

5. Joe Carroll, and Laurel Brubaker Calkins. "BP Pressured Rig Worker to Hurry Before Disaster, Father Says." *BusinessWeek*. Bloomberg, 27 May 2010. Web. 21 Sep 2010.

6. David Hammer. "Big Polluters – Oil Spill Hearings: Key Warning Systems Bypassed on Rig, Technician Testifies." *Community Center*. Np, 23 July 2010. Web. 21 Sep 2010.

7. David Hammer. "Deepwater Horizon Safety Alerts Were Bypassed to Avoid False Alarms, Witness Says." *NOLA.com*. New Orleans Net LLC., 23 July 2010. Web. 21 Sep 2010.

Chapter 5. Efforts to Stop the Oil Leak

1. Jeffrey Brown. "Coast Guard's Allen Outlines Roles of BP, Government in Gulf Oil Cleanup." *PBS: Public Broadcasting Service*. Public Broadcasting Service, 24 May 2010. Web. 21 Sep 2010.

2. Chuck Bennett. "110-ton box lowered to contain gushing oil in Gulf." *New York Post*. NYP Holdings, Inc., 8 May 2010. Web. 21 Sep 2010.

3. David Hilzenrath. "BP executive says blowout preventer was not connected properly." *Washington Post*. Washington Post Company, 25 Aug 2010. Web. 21 Sep 2010.

4. "'Relief well' to follow 'static kill' in Gulf oil spill cleanup." *CNN*. Turner Broadcasting, 6 Aug. 2010. Web. 21 Sep 2010.

SOURCE NOTES CONTINUED

Chapter 6. Environmental Effects of the Spill
1. "Signs of oil spill pollution might be hiding underwater." *Surfspots-GPS*. Np, 15 May 2010. Web. 21 Sep 2010.
2. Kaycee Lagarde, and Bill Vilona. "Oiled dolphin's rescue ends in death." *NWF Daily News*. Freedom Communications, 24 June 2010. Web. 21 Sep 2010.
3. Ibid.
4. "Is BP burning endangered sea turtles alive with oil from spill?" *Gather*. Gather Inc., Web. 20 Sep 2010.
5. "Lawsuit: Turtles Are Dying in BP Oil Burns." *CBS News*. CBS Interactive Inc., 1 July 2010. Web. 21 Sep 2010.
6. Kari Huus. "Oil dispersants an environmental 'crapshoot'." *MSNBC*. Msnbc.com, 24 May 2010. Web. 21 Sep 2010.
7. Samantha Joye. "Where has the oil gone?" *Gulf Oil Blog*. UGA, 1 Aug. 2010. Web. 21 Sep 2010.

Chapter 7. The Impact on Human Health
1. "Tests find sickened family has 50.3 ppm of Corexit's 2-butoxyethanol in swimming pool." *Florida Oil Spill Law*. FloridaOilSpillLaw.com, LLC., 30 Aug. 2010. Web. 21 Sep 2010.
2. Fred Tasker. "Gulf oil spill still a threat to seafood, JAMA study indicates." *McClatchy*. McClatchyDC.com, 17 Aug 2010. Web. 21 Sep 2010.
3. Ibid.
4. Shari Roan. "Gulf oil spill: human health effects debated." *Los Angeles Times*. Tribune Newspaper, 4 June 2010. Web. 21 Sep 2010.

Chapter 8. Financial Losses and Litigation

1. Rong-Gong Lin. "Gulf oil spill: Fishermen decry a lost season." *Los Angeles Times*. Tribune Newspaper, 31 July 2010. Web. 21 Sep 2010.

2. David Usborne. "BP hires fishermen for rig clean-up operation." *Independent*. Independent Print Limited, 3 May 2010. Web. 21 Sep 2010.

3. Rick Outzen. "BP's Windfall to the Rich." *Daily Beast*. RTST, INC., 3 June 2010. Web. 21 Sep 2010.

4. John Schwartz. "First the Spill, Then the Lawsuits." *New York Times*. New York Times Company, 10 June 2010. Web. 21 Sep. 2010.

Chapter 9. A Community under Stress

1. Lawrence Palinkas. "Psychological Impacts of Oil Spills: The Exxon Valdez Disaster." *University of Southern California*. National Academies Press, Web. 21 Sep 2010.

2. Michael Price. "A mental health crisis unfolds." *Monitor on Psychology*. APA, Sept 2010. Web. 21 Sep 2010.

3. Noel Sheppard. "White House Enacts Rules Inhibiting Media From Covering Oil Spill." *NewsBusters*. NewsBusters, 3 July 2010. Web. 21 Sep 2010.

4. "Embattled BP chief: I want my life back." *Sunday Times*. Times Newspapers Ltd., 31 May 2010. Web. 21 Sep 2010.

5. Richard Simon. "Gulf oil spill: Brother of oil-rig worker who died in explosion pleads for compensation." *Los Angeles Times*. Tribune Newspaper, 8 June 2010. Web. 21 Sep 2010.

6. "BP CEO Tony Hayward: 'I'd Like My Life Back'." *YouTube*. Np. Web. 21 Sep 2010.

7. Michael Price. "A mental health crisis unfolds." *Monitor on Psychology*. APA, Sept 2010. Web. 21 Sep 2010.

INDEX

ABOUT THE AUTHOR

Courtney Farrell is a full-time writer and the author of a dozen books for young people. She is interested in conservation, social justice, and sustainability issues. She lives with her husband and sons on a ranch in the Colorado mountains.

PHOTO CREDITS